MUNICIPAL BUSES OF THE 1960s

MUNICIPAL BUSES
OF THE 1960s

LYNDON W. ROWE

D. BRADFORD BARTON LTD

Frontispiece:
St. Helens Corporation Leyland PD2/20 No. F117 outside Shaw Street Garage in May 1965. Built new in 1956, the bodywork is by Weymann.

Published by Enterprise Transport Books Ltd
3 Barnsway, Kings Langley, Hertfordshire WD4 9PW

Printed and bound in Great Britain by BPC Hazell Books Ltd

Seen against the dignified background of Stormont Buildings, a Belfast Corporation Daimler Fleetline leaves the grounds of Parliament to return to City Hall. No.584 has bodywork by M H Coachworks and was delivered in 1962. It was photographed in June 1964 when working former trolleybus Route 23.

introduction

Although several pictorial books have been published which deal with various aspects of passenger road transport, it is perhaps still the exception for the municipal operator to receive as much attention as area agreement companies, or even the independent side of the bus industry. When the municipal scene has been brought into focus, it has usually been in regard to the larger fleets operating in cities such as Birmingham, Manchester or Sheffield, whilst the medium-sized and smaller operators have received but passing attention.

This volume deliberately pays less attention to the giants of the industry, and whilst the reader will find all municipal operators in these islands represented at least once herein, the major organisations are found less frequently than some of the smaller undertakings. Out of the 96 operators illustrated, one or two may perhaps appear to receive over-much attention, but this is because their fleets are of varied or significant interest.

One of the key omissions is made obvious by the title, which relates to buses and does not include trolleybuses or trams. Trams were present at Blackpool throughout the decade, and trolleybuses were of course still in evidence in a number of towns covered in this book, their wires appearing in many of the photographs. A decision was taken, however, to devote a separate volume to trolleybuses, and I must assure the many friends and supporters of electric traction that far from slighting the smooth, silent vehicle, I have deliberately ensured that they will have a more abundant pictorial feast at a later date.

The period covered by this volume is the decade which commenced in 1960. By that year the private car had made its mark on traditional municipal bus traffics, which had declined by around 15 per cent in the previous decade, but the passenger vehicles themselves – of which some 19,000 existed in 1960 – were still following the basic patterns of earlier times with the revolutionary rear-engined Atlantean only just beginning to enter service. Wallasey Corporation had taken delivery of the first examples in municipal service in 1958, but the new idea was relatively slow to catch on, and at the start of the decade the later rush to one-man operation had yet to gain momentum.

Drivers and conductors were the regular custodians of vehicles on the urban scene at the start of our period, and the vehicles which they operated were often of a longevity which, some twenty years later, must seem strange to the younger enthusiast. By the end of the period much one-man operation was commonplace, and the influx of new vehicles into fleets had materially decreased the average age. Whether the comfort experienced by a passenger is greater in one of today's rear-engined vehicles than in a Leyland-bodied PD2 of earlier times must be a matter of conjecture, but it is surprising to recall that few vehicles twenty years ago had heaters fitted, and most had open platforms – yet the passengers of that era did not seem to find the environment too unpleasant, even during severe winters like that of 1963.

The municipal bus has, by its nature, been primarily a high-capacity vehicle, and by tradition this has made double-decker operation more commonplace than single-decker. In the 1960s only the small fleets at Colwyn Bay and Llandudno were entirely single-decker operations, whilst some fleets, for example Derby, Hartlepool, or Plymouth, possessed purely double-decker vehicles. This emphasis on the double-decker bus had begun to change during the decade, as the need for economy forced managements to look to the single-decker as a means of one-man operation, although the clearance for one-man operated double-decker vehicles eventually reversed this trend.

The decade depicted saw the decline of the trolleybus within the United Kingdom, and also saw dramatic social changes. At its close it saw the planned demise of many of the operators depicted in these pages with the formation of the Passenger Transport Executives in Selnec and Merseyside, later to be followed by West Yorkshire, South Yorkshire and the various amalgamations of smaller authorities under the District Councils.

Some have since altered their names and liveries but otherwise remain virtually unchanged.

The photographs used herein are entirely taken from my own collection and were all taken in the decade under notice. I have taken the rare step of including the month and year in which each photograph was taken in the caption as this adds to the interest. The vehicles depicted have been arranged in approximate order of their entry to service, and have been selected to show the varied nature of the municipal scene. The major problem involved was what to omit, and I must apologise if anyone feels that his favourite vehicle type has not been represented. Considerations of space forced me to leave out numerous examples which I would have liked to include, but those chosen make up the scene as a whole although I am well conscious, for example, that the inclusion of a single Leyland Atlantean is not truly representative of a fleet such as Nottingham City Transport. The large number of Leyland PD2s included reflects the fact that Leyland had by far the largest share of the market, rather than demonstrating any bias on my own part against other manufacturers.

This volume then is dedicated to the many undertakings whose operations are by and large taken for granted, and to those numerous dedicated Transport Managers who have battled frequently with their political masters on local councils to provide the public with a service that is both efficient and economic. Some undertakings were a byword for efficiency, and Leicester City Transport is an obvious candidate for this praise. Some were known for the superb external appearance of their vehicles – Southport coming immediately to mind in this connection. All have contributed greatly to mobility in the urban areas which they served, and their varied liveries added a colour to life in our cities which, regretfully, has been reduced in recent years by amalgamations and by the drab liveries adopted by the vehicles of the National Bus Company. A further loss has frequently been the municipal coat of arms which for years graced the sides of most vehicles – something which demonstrated a pride in local ownership which no passing 'logo' has achieved in the current decade.

Lastly I would like to acknowledge the assistance given in preparing this volume by my brother, Trevor Rowe, who printed the photographs and also helped greatly with its compilation.

Lyndon W. Rowe

Amongst the oldest vehicles still to be seen on the roads in the 1960s were some pre-war chassis which had received modified bodies in the post-war period. Although no longer in passenger service by May 1963, when this photograph was taken at London Road Garage, Southend Corporation No.203 is typical of this practice. This A E C Regal was delivered new in 1930 with English Electric bodywork, and was extensively rebuilt by Southend Corporation in 1955. It was finally withdrawn and sold for scrap in 1968.

Open-top vehicles are well known for their longevity, since their restricted seasons of operation are often further curtailed by wet weather. On a sunny day in October 1963, a Leyland TD3 of Southport Corporation takes the air at the Monument. The vehicle, with English Electric bodywork, dates from 1934.

English Electric bodywork again features on this Leyland TD4 of Portsmouth Corporation photographed in August 1963, conveying summer trippers bound for Clarence Pier. No. 5 was delivered new to the Corporation as a closed-top vehicle in 1935. It was one of four of the type converted to open-top between 1953 and 1955.

As a contrast to the open-top vehicles, this Leyland TD4, delivered to Portsmouth Corporation in the same year, has Leyland bodywork. Seen at Portsmouth Dockyard in August 1963, it proves that heavy all-the-year-round use of vehicles does not always lead to retirement at an early age.

In 1903 Eastbourne was the first local authority to introduce a municipal bus service, and has always been renowned for the high standard of appearance set by its fleet. Although mainly an operator of double-decker vehicles, two single-decker buses of special interest remained in use in the period covered by this book. No. 12, a Leyland Lion LT9 with Leyland bodywork, dates from 1939 and was converted from petrol to diesel operation as late as 1954. The A E C Regal dates from 1950, and both vehicles are now preserved, having remained in use at Eastbourne until 1967 and 1976 respectively. The scene is Churchdale Road Garage in September 1965.

The year 1937 saw delivery to Stockport Corporation of twenty Leyland Tiger TS7 chassis with English Electric bodywork. These twenty had centre entrances and were quite elegant in appearance. By 1961 the numbers in active service were dwindling, but No. 188 is seen in September of that year reversing in a quiet cul-de-sac at Cheadle Heath, before returning to Stockport Mersey Square.

Few towns followed the railway practice of naming locomotives by giving titles to their bus fleets, but Eastbourne Corporation was one exception. 'The White Knight', actually fleet No. 10, is an A E C Regent II with Northern Counties body and dates from 1938. Seen in May 1961 at Eastbourne Pier, it is employed on the Sea Front Service 6, and offered one hour's ride for the bargain price of one shilling and sixpence.

Morecambe and Heysham Corporation
has always found a use for open-top
vehicles operating on a route from Battery
to Bare via the promenade. No.25, seen
here in June 1965, is an A E C Regent I with
Park Royal bodywork, and was delivered
in 1938. Note the windshield on the upper
deck, and compare it with the more
spartan vehicles in the earlier pages.

One of the most elegant bodies
constructed for double-decker buses was
that produced by Weymann in the
immediate pre-war and post-war periods.
Representing the former period, Brighton
Corporation No.60, an A E C Regent I of
1939, waits for both two- and four-legged
passengers to board whilst working Town
Circular 42 at Brighton station in May
1964.

The Isle of Man possessed only a single municipal operator, and this, Douglas Corporation, will appear from time to time in these pages because of the interst and variety of its fleet. In July 1966, A E C Regent I No.50 is seen waiting another turn of duty at Victoria Pier Bus Station. Delivered in 1939, this vehicle was equipped with a Northern Counties body, and was the last of its batch to survive in service in the island, being sold for preservation on the mainland in 1967.

VICTORIA PIER

DOUGLAS CORPORATION TRANSPORT

50

DMN 650

Quite a number of buses delivered with utility bodywork during the Second World War were subsequently rebodied, and saw many years of useful service. This Daimler CWG5 of Lancaster City Transport first saw service in 1943, but was rebodied by Crossley in 1952. It is seen in June 1965 in Lancaster Bus Station on Route W.

Amongst the largest operators in the municipal field, Manchester Corporation Transport Department was a great support of Daimler chassis. No. 4266, a COG5 with Met-Cammell bodywork, negotiates the street of Didsbury on a foggy December day in 1961 whilst working a farewell tour for the P S V Circle. It entered service in 1940.

Luton Corporation ceased to be a public service vehicle operator in 1970, but before its demise was unusual in possessing a batch of low bridge double-decker vehicles acquired from United Counties in 1961. This Bristol K5G with Eastern Coachworks bodywork is leaving Park Street Garage, and was supplied new to United Counties in 1940. The livery of dull red did little to brighten up the showery day in April 1963 when this photograph was taken.

Various operators acquired the famous Bedford OWB, which was manufactured in great quantities in World War II, although municipal fleets were not amongst the more usual customers. Portsmouth Corporation had ten such vehicles, and No. 169 is seen at Cosham Post Office en route to Wymering in May 1962. New in 1944, the body was built by Duple.

Mergers between municipal operators did not become commonplace until it became fashionable to alter local authority boundaries in the 1970s. Where towns were close together, however, it made little economic sense to continue to operate individual public transport departments, Grimsby and Cleethorpes being one example of a merger which took place in 1957. This Guy Arab II was originally part of the Grimsby Corporation fleet, and is seen at Riby Square in June 1965. No. 87 dates from 1944, and has a Roe 61-seat body provided in 1958.

Some municipal operations were on a small scale when compared with their larger brethren, and Lowestoft Corporation concentrated its vehicles on one major trunk route through the town centre. The fleet was housed in an ex-tramway depot in Rotterdam Road, and traces of the tramway track can still be seen in this view of Guy Arab No.6 resting in the tight confines of the depot in August 1964. Delivered in 1945, the vehicle was equipped with bodywork by Massey.

Belfast Corporation was a stronghold of Daimler vehicles and many saw years of service. Daimler CWA6 No.214 was first delivered in 1944, and although the Harkness bodywork was rebuilt by the Corporation in 1950, the vehicle was still going strong in June 1964 when passing the City Hall on Route 28.

Essex has only two municipal operators, and Colchester Corporation possessed some interesting vehicles in the period under review. Five Bristol K6A dating from 1945 were equipped with bodies by Duple or Park Royal, and one of the former batch is seen here ascending North Hill in August 1962 bound for Monkwick Estate.

The Park Royal bodies are represented by No. 47, photographed at the John Kent Avenue terminus in March 1962.

So far we have visited municipal operators in England, Northern Ireland and the Isle of Man, but it is in Wales that Pontypridd Urban District Council operated this Guy Arab II with Northern Counties bodywork, a vehicle dating from 1945 and seen here waiting for passengers at Cilfynydd Colliery in April 1965. It was withdrawn from service and sold for scrap some eight months later.

Pontypridd made use of a substantial fleet of double-deck vehicles on Bristol or Guy chassis, and a line-up is seen at the depot in September 1964. The Bristol nearest the camera is a K6A with Park Royal body and dates from 1945, whilst its neighbour is a K5G. In the far background, Guy Arab LUF No. 77 looks almost irritable at its failure to be in the limelight.

The largest bus operator in the United Kingdom is of course London Transport, and former LT buses sometimes found new homes with municipal bus fleets. Burton-on-Trent acquired six Guy Arab II with Park Royal utility bodies in 1953. New to the L P T B in 1945 as G324, Burton No.65 was still largely in original condition when recorded in May 1963 at the Town Hall. It was withdrawn at the end of the following year.

Lincoln is the setting for this Leyland PD1 with Roe bodywork dating from 1946. One of a batch of five vehicles, it is here seen in June 1963 passing beneath the historic Stonebow in Lincoln High Street.

By the 1960s wooden slatted seats had all but gone from passenger vehicles, but exceptions did still exist, as demonstrated by this view inside a Duple-bodied Daimler CWA6 owned by Douglas Corporation. The photograph was taken in September 1967, but the spartan seating lasted until the vehicle was withdrawn some three years later. The Daimler, new in 1946, is working the promenade service and is seen at Derby Castle with the Corporation Horse Tram depot on the left.

Morecambe promenade is again
the scene for our visit to
Morecambe and Heysham
Corporation. These A E C
Regent II vehicles with Park
Royal bodywork were supplied in
1947, and were still active in
September 1965 when the
photograph was taken.

In 1961 roadworks in
Wolverhampton led to the
replacement of certain trolleybus
routes by motor buses, and to
assist with the extra demand for
the latter the Corporation
arranged loans from Birmingham
City Transport. No.1573, a
Daimler CVG6 with
Met-Cammell body, is seen in
Chubb Street, Wolverhampton,
whilst working Route 4. The bus
dates from 1947.

Eastern Coachworks bodywork was never a regular feature of municipal operations, but one particular exception was a batch of nine vehicles supplied to Lowestoft Corporation in 1947. Mounted on A E C Regent chassis, these buses were justly renowned in later years amongst vehicle enthusiasts. In September 1963, Regent No. 25 is passing Sparrows Nest Lighthouse en route to Pakefield.

Leeds City Transport possessed a
considerable fleet of A E C Regent
IIIs, and No. 431 represents a
batch of 72 delivered with Roe
bodywork in 1947. It is shown
entering the Central Bus Station
in October 1963 on Route 35.

No more typical example of the
important role played by Crossley
in the municipal scene could be
found to illustrate their products
than this DD42 of Manchester
Corporation, seen at Third
Avenue on Trafford Park
Industrial Estate in March 1963.
No. 2219 is the last of a batch of
220 delivered to the Corporation
and entered service in 1947, with
bodywork by Crossley. Note the
large oval bus stop plate used by
M C T D.

Perhaps the most unusual vehicle illustrated in this volume is this Bedford QL of Southport Corporation, operating on a service across the extensive sands for which this Lancashire resort is well known. Delivered in 1947, these vehicles were army lorries converted by Rimmer, Harrison & Sutherland, and carried 23 passengers. Although not licensed as public service vehicles, these 'lorries' provided a service between Southport Pier and Ainsdale Beach. No.13 is seen at Southport Pier in June 1965.

The only municipal operation in Kent is confined to the County Town itself, Maidstone. In 1947 a batch of three Daimler CVG6 vehicles were purchased, with bodywork by Northern Coachbuilders. One of these, No.75, is seen at London Road, Allington Way, in April 1962 in the ochre-and-cream livery then in use. This vehicle survived to be the only Daimler to carry the current blue-and-cream livery, and was withdrawn in 1968.

Petrol vehicles were a rarity in 1961, but three still existed at Reading; one of this trio was No.71, seen parked outside Mill Lane depot in June of that year. These buses were the survivors of a batch delivered in 1947, and Mulliner bodywork was provided on Bedford OB chassis. No.71 was eventually withdrawn in September 1963.

Aberdare Urban District Council was a further operator using Eastern Coachworks bodywork, but this time on the more usual Bristol K6A chassis. Introduced in 1947 as fleet No. 44, this vehicle was later renumbered 77, and is seen in August 1962 in the town centre. It was withdrawn and sold for scrap some three years later.

Ashton-under-Lyme Corporation lost its individual identity when the South East Lancashire; North East Cheshire Passenger Transport Executive was formed, but in its day the blue-and-cream livery made an attractive sight in the industrial areas served. Seen here at Ashton Market Place in March 1963, Leyland PD1 No. 44 is provided with Crossley bodywork and was turned out in 1947.

Virtually every book on buses includes the famous London RT Class. Few were sold to municipal operators, although some of them, with Craven bodies, did see service in Dundee for some years. Some RT vehicles did not travel so far north, however, and Bradford Corporation No. 403, formerly RT No. 158, is seen at Exchange station in May 1964. The bodywork was by Weymann and the bus was delivered new to London Transport in 1947, with whom it served for eleven years.

Two examples of A E C RT chassis were purchased new by Douglas in 1947, and were provided with Northern Counties bodywork. No. 54 has just arrived at the Jubilee Clock Tower in Douglas, and passes Horse Tram No. 44 – on which the Queen Mother once rode (note the royal crest on the roof canopy). Although the date is July 1966, the scene has changed little over the years, but whilst Douglas Corporation buses are now but a memory, the horse tramway still continues as a profitable public transport enterprise. No. 54 saw service in Douglas until 1971.

This Leyland PD1 with Weymann body (new in 1948) represents the post-war delivery of buses to Portsmouth Corporation, and is seen at Floating Bridge terminus in March 1961. Route Number 145 (previously R/S) looks slightly strange in comparison with the letters at one time found on Portsmouth screens.

A casualty in the list
operators was West
Bridgford
Corporation, whose
services were
absorbed by
Nottingham in 1968
A E C No.5 is a
Regent III dating fro
1948 and is equipped
with Park Royal
bodywork. This
scene, dating from
August 1965, was
taken near
Nottingham Midlan
station.

Although a rare type in municipal bus operations, a few authorities did operate Foden vehicles, including Chester, which used them for many years. In the pleasant setting of one of England's most historic cities, No. 73 waits for passengers outside Chester City Hall in July 1961. This Foden PVD6 is provided with Massey bodywork and entered service in 1948.

The timbered housing behind Coventry Corporation No. 61 shows that this heavily damaged city was not entirely destroyed in World War II. This Daimler CVA6 with Met-Cammell body was one of 96 of the type, and was delivered new in 1949. It is seen in the city centre in May 1963. Both Coventry Corporation and Timothy Whites were to be the subject of takeovers in later years.

One of the most interesting of the smaller municipal fleets was that at Todmorden on the Lancashire–Yorkshire border. The Joint Omnibus Committee was operated by Todmorden Corporation and British Railways, and some of the buses possessed a railway flavour, with interior signs reading 'No Smoking in this Compartment'. Todmorden was the first purchaser of production Leyland PD2/1 vehicles and No. 36 dates from 1948; it has Leyland bodywork and is seen at the bus station beneath the former Lancashire & Yorkshire Railway viaduct in Todmorden. Although the photograph was taken in September 1964, the crest on the vehicle side still attributes part ownership to the L M S Railway.

Reading provides the setting for this A E C Regent II with Park Royal bodywork, en route for the trolleybus terminus at Kentwood in March 1964. The vehicle was new in 1948.

Although dating from 1948, this Daimler CVG6 with Met-Cammell body looks somewhat older. It is entering the Oak Lane Garage of West Bromwich Corporation in August 1963.

Lincoln Corporation No. 23 was a Guy Arab III, with bodywork by the same manufacturer, and entered service in 1948. It was later fitted experimentally with a Ruston & Hornsby air-cooled engine, and is seen outside Lincoln Central station in June 1963.

Yet another operator destined to vanish in later years was Lytham St. Annes, although in this case the change involved the name only. Lytham is here represented by a Leyland PD2/1 of 1948 with Leyland bodywork, caught by the camera outside the Lytham Garage, near Squires Gate, in September 1965. This garage once saw duty as a tramway depot.

Throughout the years, Leicester City Transport has been regarded as the model of a well-organised municipal operator, and this fact is as true today as when No. 18 was photographed outside St. Margarets Bus Station in May 1965. This A E C Regent III was one of 65 supplied new to the Transport Department in 1948, and was provided with Brush bodywork.

Along with Chester, Warrington Corporation was also a purchaser of Foden vehicles, and No. 40 was one of a batch of five delivered in 1949 with East Lancashire bodywork. The vehicle is leaving the Warrington Garage at Wilderspool Causeway; March 1963.

Haslingden Corporation possessed four Leyland PS2/1 chassis with Burlingham bodies, and the highest numbered of these is seen leaving the Haslingden garage in John Street in September 1965. The small garage is identified by the double-decker Leyland also entering service for the late afternoon peak workings. The PS2 vehicles were new in 1948.

Exeter is yet another operator to vanish with the passing of time, and Daimler CVD6 No. 173 of 1949 stands next to a representative of the company which was eventually to absorb the municipal service. Seen at Paul Street in April 1964, the Daimler has Weymann bodywork, and an example of this class of vehicle has now been preserved.

Much has changed since this photograph was taken at Stepney level crossing in Kingston-upon-Hull in March 1962. The gates are about to close as A E C Regent III No.326 passes through on Route 17. This bus was one of 55 of its type purchased new in 1949-50, and fitted with the handsome Weymann bodywork on offer at that time.

The operations of Gelligaer Urban District Council were confined to the area around Bargoed, and double-deckers operated the trunk service from Ystrad Mynach to Bargoed. New in 1949, this A E C Regent III with Bruce low-height body on East Lancashire frames is passing beneath the railway viaduct near Bargoed in October 1963. It was withdrawn from service in 1965.

Crossley bodywork on Guy Arab III chassis was fairly uncommon. This example was operated by Blackburn and is bound for Cherry Tree in May 1965. Compare the appearance of the bodywork, here in dark green-and-cream livery, with that on the Ashton vehicle in blue-and-cream illustrated on page 27.

Northampton Corporation operated Crossley DD42 and Daimler CVD6 chassis with Roe bodywork. One of the former, new in 1946, is No. 149, which stands at the town centre in February 1962 and is typical of the Northampton fleet at that time.

Newcastle Corporation vehicles were provided with a bright canary livery, and a large fleet served the needs of this important north-east city. Representative of a small batch of Leyland PD2/1 vehicles with Leyland bodies delivered in 1949, No. 356 waits outside the Central Library in April 1963. It was originally numbered 8.

Rawthenstall Corporation in Lancashire operated ten Leyland PD2/1 with Leyland bodywork, delivered in 1949; No. 3 is seen in Market Street, Bury, in May 1965.

As mentioned earlier, 30 A E C RT type buses with Craven bodywork were sold to Dundee Corporation by London Transport in 1956. Seen here in Princes Street, Dundee, former RT No. 1459 and RT No. 1428 have both been modified to show the ultimate destination only, but are otherwise basically as delivered to London Transport in 1949. When this photograph was taken in April 1964, these RTs had served longer north of the border than south of it.

Birmingham City Transport operated a large number of Crossley vehicles, with bodywork by the same manufacturer. Introduced to service in 1949, No.2384 is seen in September 1966 at Bournville whilst working the outer circle service.

An example of Crossley chassis and bodywork for a single-decker is Bolton Corporation No. 7, seen outside the garage in September 1962. This particular vehicle was one of a batch of four delivered in 1949.

The only Leyland Comet buses to serve in a municipal fleet in Britain were three CPO1 type supplied to Douglas in 1950 and equipped with Park Royal 30-seat bodies. No. 21 is at Victoria Pier Bus Station in July 1966. These vehicles were the only home-operated Comet buses to be bodied by Park Royal.

Darwen Corporation No. 43 w
formerly a Crossley
demonstration bus, but entere
service at Darwen in 1951. Th
scene is Belgrave Road in
Darwen, and the bus is bound
Blackburn on the joint service
July 1963. Bodywork is once
again by Crossley.

Blackpool Corporation possessed
a fleet of one hundred Leyland
PD2/5 vehicles with unusual
centre-entrance bodies by
Burlingham. Introduced in 1949,
No. 244 is seen near Blackpool
Tower in September 1965, and is
surrounded by the illuminations
for which this seaside resort is
justly famous.

Vehicles acquired by municipal operators from London Transport have already been illustrated. In 1963, however, Southport Corporation obtained three Leyland Tiger PS2 buses with Burlingham bodies from Ribble Motor Services, and converted them for seafront use as open vehicles. New in 1950, No. 10 is seen in June 1965 in Southport en route to Botanic Gardens. Although No. 10 had departed, its two sisters were still in service at Southport in 1978.

This book would not be truly representative of the Glasgow Corporation fleet without the presence of an Albion Venturer, and this Roberts–bodied example is at Carntyne station in June 1961. The vehicle formed one of a batch of 40 supplied new in 1949.

Oldham Corporation was another user of route letters, as shown by this March 1963 photograph of a Crossley SD42/7 with Roe bodywork on Route E. The location is Oldham Town Hall, and the vehicle dates from 1950.

By way of contrast, this lower illustration shows the single-decker equivalent of the type above right. New in 1950, No. 445 is also a Daimler CVG6, but has Burlingham bodywork with a rear entrance, this latter destined to become rare on single-decker buses. The scene is again the Bus Station at Manchester Exchange, September 1961. In both photographs, note the destination winding gear employed by Salford on double-decker vehicles.

One of the municipal bus fleets to shun external advertising was Salford City Transport, and the city crest positioned between the decks endowed the buses with a distinctive and dignified appearance. Salford operated many Daimler CVG6 vehicles with Met-Cammell bodywork, and this scene shows Nos. 493 and 498, both new in 1951, at the Salford Bus Station adjacent to Manchester Exchange; September 1962.

In Preston both systems of route identification are used, since the destination screens can carry both numbers and letters. Leyland PD2/10 No. 46, photographed in September 1967, is painted in the new blue livery which at that date was beginning to replace the former deep crimson and cream. The Leyland bodywork is standard for 1952, when the vehicle was delivered.

There is still a vaguely utility look about this Eastern Coachworks body supplied new in 1950 to Middlesbrough Corporation, and placed on Guy Arab III chassis. Seen in Stockton in September 1965, this vehicle is in the pleasing blue livery used by Middlesbrough, and contrasts with the Stockton example below.

Stockton Corporation operated this Leyland PD2/3 with Weymann bodywork delivered new in 1950. The vehicle begins to look somewhat elderly when seen in the High Street in September 1965, but the overall appearance is not helped by the drab green livery adopted by the Corporation.

Ipswich did not operate buses until 1950, and the first batch of vehicles purchased were six A E C Regent III with bodywork by Park Royal. No.5, leaving Lloyds Avenue in the town centre in April 1961, is bound for the railway station. The trolleybus wires demonstrate the method of public transport in Ipswich soon to be replaced by the diesel bus.

To represent the most northerly municipality included in these pages is Aberdeen No.166, a Daimler CVG6 delivered in 1951, but here portrayed with Alexander body dating from 1960. The location is King Street in September 1965, and the well-kept Daimler is bound for Garthdee.

Another A E C Regent III, this time with bodywork by Weymann, in George Square, Glasgow, in April 1962. The bus was one of a batch of a hundred delivered in 1951.

Glasgow Corporation was a great Daimler stronghold for many years although it shared its favours widely amongst the available manufacturers. Alexander bodywork was also a familiar item, and No.D21, seen outside St. Enoch station in April 1962, has this make of body on CVD6 chassis. The vehicle dates from 1950 and provides a contrast of livery and style with the later buses on the loading islands in the background.

At the opposite end of the scale from the large network operated by Glasgow is the small organisation in South Wales of Bedwas and Machen Urban District Council, for many years possessing three vehicles only. One of the two A E C Regal III buses with bodywork by Bruce, No. 7 is seen passing the Boars Head Tavern opposite the castle at Caerphilly in June 1963. The vehicle dates from 1951.

Centre entrances have been rare in these pages so far, and this combination of Bristol L5G chassis with East Lancashire (Bridlington) bodywork is a particularly unusual example. No. 117 of Rotherham Corporation is standing in the yard at Rawmarsh Road Garage in July 1962. Delivered new in 1950, No. 117 was the first of a batch of six such vehicles.

The use of Leyland Royal Tiger chassis is more usually associated with company operators, but this example, with Leyland body, was purchased in 1952 by Widnes Corporation. Seen in September 1966 outside the Widnes garage.

Centre-entrance buses were also employed in Darlington, and this Guy Arab III has Roe bodywork and dates from 1952. The location is Bank Top station, April 1964.

Barrow-in-Furness is the home of this Leyland PD2/3 with Park Royal bodywork delivered in 1950; September 1965.

With the longest name in municipal transport in this country, the Stalybridge, Hyde, Mossley and Dukinfield Transport and Electricity Board – more usually known as S H M D – operated a varied fleet of interesting vehicles. Representing the 1952 series of Daimler CVD6, No.62 has Northern Counties bodywork and is passing Marple station in October 1963.

Apart from London Transport, Coventry and Douglas, A E C RT vehicles were also supplied new to St. Helens Corporation. Purchased in 1952, they operated for ten years before being sold to Kingston-upon-Hull in 1962. In the later guise as Hull No. 137, this Park Royal-bodied example is leaving the garage to take up an afternoon turn of duty on Route 92 in May 1964.

The sole RT supplied to Coventry Corporation was numbered 99, and entered service in 1951. Seen here in May 1963, it heads a long procession of buses in the afternoon peak hour at the junction of Priory Street and Ford Street. The Met-Cammell body is to the basic London design, including the RT number plate on the bonnet.

Todmorden No. 27 is a Leyland PD2/12 with Leyland 8' wide body, and was recorded in September 1965 leaving the town bus station for the long climb to the terminus at Summit. This bus was delivered new in 1951.

Widnes Corporation No. 17 is a Leyland-bodied PD2/12 dating from 1952, and is seen outside the municipal bus garage at St. Helens in June 1965. Note the window opening on the near side only on the upper deck.

Rochdale Corporation is represented by A E C Regent III No. 226, one of a batch with Weymann bodywork delivered new in 1950 and seen in Rochdale town centre in March 1963.

Another example of the Birmingham City Transport fleet, this time a Daimler CVD6 with Met-Cammell body. No. 2708 is one of 150 such buses which began delivery in 1951; photographed on Route 15 near New Street station, March 1967.

One of the most spectacular municipal routes was that of the West Monmouthshire Omnibus Board between Bargoed and Markham. The route involved tight corners, a hill of momentous steepness with 250′ at 1 in 4¼, 500′ at 1 in 5 and 1220′ at 1 in 8, plus a very low railway bridge. No. 13 is negotiating this obstacle course in September 1963, having been built in 1959 with a Willowbrook body. The Leyland chassis was a modified PD2/38 fitted with sprag gear to prevent backward running; it was rebodied as a double-decker in 1966 after the route had been diverted from Bargoed Hill.

The tortuous nature of the route is furthe[r] demonstrated by Foden PVSO6 No.30 (new in 1952) which, despite the destination shown, is bound for Bargoe[d]. The bodywork is again by Willowbroo[k]

West Monmouthshire was also the owner of this A E C Monocoach with Park Royal body, which had formerly served as a demonstration bus with London Transport. Built in 1955, it is seen ten years later in October 1965 at Blackwood Garage.

In North Wales, it was possible to see further examples of Foden single-decker buses in daily use, and this one, dating from 1951, has Metalcraft bodywork. Owned by Llandudno Urban District Council, it is bound for the Great Orme and is seen in Prospect Terrace shortly before crossing the Great Orme Tramway. These Fodens were fitted with drag equipment and low ratio gears for the steep climb to the Orme; September 1966.

A Roe-bodied Guy Arab IV of 1954 operated by South Shield Corporation. It is here seen in training drivers for the forthcoming conversion of the remaining trolleybus routes; Marsden Inn, April 1963.

Ramsbottom Urban District Council, in Lancashire, operated this 1952 Leyland-bodied Roy Tiger, photographed passing over the level crossing by the local station in May 1965. Compare this off side view with that of the near side of Widnes No. 18 on page 53.

Wallasey Corporation Motors
was a most interesting operator to
the enthusiast, as it used a
traditional form of fleet name
display on the side of its buses,
and also included a clock face on
the rear platform to indicate ferry
connections at Seacombe.
Leaving New Brighton terminus
in September 1964, No. 55 is an
example of Met-Cammell
bodywork on Leyland PD2/1
chassis.

Brush bodywork was used on a
number of vehicles owned by
Derby Corporation, including
this Foden PVD6 of 1952; Derby
Bus Station, May 1963.

In 1953 London Transport took delivery of 84 Guy Special chassis with bodywork by Eastern Coachworks, and these 26-seat buses were used as replacements for Leyland Cubs. The development of one-man operation on the larger RF Class, however, made many of these Guy vehicles redundant, and in 1961 Nos. GS40 and GS41 were sold to West Bromwich Corporation. No. 233 (formerly No. GS41), at Dudley Bus Station in October 1964, shows how the smart West Bromwich livery blended well with the lines of these very handsome buses.

One of the smallest operators included in these pages is Colwyn Bay, which has used a small fleet of buses on a promenade service in the North Wales seaside town since 1926. Introduced to service in 1954, No. 1 in the fleet is a Bedford with 21-seat bodywork by Spurling; photographed at Colwyn Bay Pier in September 1966.

An A E C Regal IV with Weymann body owned by Dundee Corporation. The appearance is similar to the London Transport RF Class concurrently being delivered in 1953. The passengers are boarding Route 3 at a stop in Crichton Street in April 1964.

A well-known manufacturer that has not so far appeared in these pages is Dennis Bros. of Guildford. In 1954 this Dennis Falcon L9 was put into service by Newport Corporation and Davies bodywork was provided on Park Royal frames. Seen at Newport Bus Station in April 1966, this vehicle was one of many interesting Dennis single-deckers at that time in Newport ownership.

When Southampton Corporation tramways were converted to bus operation, a large fleet of Guy Arabs with Park Royal bodywork was obtained. No. 71 was one of a later batch delivered in 1954 to the same basic design as earlier models, and is seen in London Road in April 1964 on Route 14. Note the experimental ventilation system on either side of the destination screen.

Southend Corporation was a traditional user of vehicles built to low height specifications, and this Leyland PD2/20 with Weymann body was introduced to service in 1954; No. 284 waits for prospective passengers outside Southend Victoria station in May 1963.

A typical Edinburgh Corporation
vehicle of the period is this Guy
Arab IV with Alexander
bodywork, new in 1955. No.915
is ascending the Mound bound for
Morningside on Route 23. May
1965.

Also new in 1955 was this A E C
Regent V of Doncaster
Corporation, seen near the
railway station in May 1964;
bodywork is by Roe.

East Lancashire bodywork graces this Leyland PD2/12 of Burnley, Colne & Nelson, seen leaving Burnley Bus Station in September 1965. Bound for the foreboding destination of Bleak House, No. 220 was one of a batch of six supplied new in 1955.

Liverpool No. L161 is a Leyland PD2/20 with Alexander body, and dates from 1954. The scene i Pier Head in July 1966, and the vehicle is employed on the city circle service.

In the 1960s Liverpool operated a special Airport Service between Lime Street station and Speke Airport, four Leyland Royal Tiger PSU1/13 coaches with half-decker bodies by Met-Cammell being employed to work it. These four dated from 1956 but were rebuilt in 1961; No. XL173 is seen outside Lime Street in May 1965 waiting for connecting passengers.

A type of bodywork produced in great quantities by Met-Cammell was the lightweight 'Orion', and an example on Leyland PD2/12 chassis is seen in September 1961 in the Manchester suburb of West Didsbury. M C T D No. 3466 was new in 1956.

A 1957-built example of an A E C Regent V with Park Royal body, waiting alongside an earlier Met-Cammell-bodied Daimler at Castle Street terminus in Aberdeen; September 1965.

An interesting scene at Shrubhill Works, Edinburgh, in June 1960 shows Leyland PD3/2 No.998 flanked by the Guy Wulfrunian demonstrator and Leyland PD3 No.999. Both Edinburgh vehicles possess bodywork by Alexanders, No.998 having been exhibited at the Scottish Show in 1957, and No.999 being new some two years later. The Wulfrunian was built in 1960, and was the third chassis of this type to be constructed.

Darwen No. 17, a Crossley Regent V dating from 1957 and equipped with bodywork by East Lancashire. Recorded at Darwen Circus in September 1965, the destination screen suggests that Crossley supporters could be en route to lobby their MP. No. 17 was the last vehicle of double-decker design to be produced under the Crossley name.

st Lancashire bodywork also tures on this 1956 single-decker y Arab LUF of Accrington rporation. Accrington ssessed three of these eresting vehicles, and they ked smart in the unusual deep e and red livery favoured by ir owners. Bound for Green worth, No. 16 is seen in crington town centre in ptember 1965.

Met-Cammell-bodied
Leyland PD2/40
No. 100 of Plymouth
Corporation, dating
from 1958, seen
passing beneath the
Western Region tracks
of British Railways at
North Road station in
April 1964.

Until August 1953,
operation between
Hartlepool and West
Hartlepool had been
undertaken by
trolleybuses of West
Hartlepool
Corporation, but
from that date
Hartlepool put four
ex-London Transport
Bristols into service.
In 1956 these gave way
to A E C Regent V
chassis with Roe
bodywork, and No. 1
is seen at the
Hartlepool terminus
in September 1965.

Lincoln is a city of great historical interest, and also provides excellent scenes for bus photography. Here, Leyland PD2/31 No. 79 of 1957 passes through the Eastgate in May 1965 on the way to Boultham Moor; bodywork is by Roe.

The livery on this 1957 Met-Cammell-bodied Leyland PD2/40 of Portsmouth Corporation makes an interesting contrast to that on the M C T D and Plymouth examples already seen. No. 115 speeds along Festing Road in Southsea on Route B in May 1962.

Rotherham Corporation employed a small batch of Daimler CVG6 vehicles with lo height bodywork by Roe. First introduced into service in 1957, No. 132 is at All Saints Square in August 1967 when working Route 33 to the Three Magpies Hotel.

A batch of Leyland PD2/30 chassis was equipped with Weymann bodywork and delivered to Chesterfield Corporation in 1958; No.207 heads along Sheffield Road towards the town centre in December 1963.

Whilst a number of operators purchased the Dennis Loline to gain experience of the type, it never made a marked impact in municipal service. One operator which purchased two examples in 1958 was Leigh Corporation, and both were given bodies by East Lancashire. No.63 is at Leigh Bus Station in July 1963.

The year 1958 saw the introduction to municipal service of the new concept in double-decker design which was to have a far-reaching effect upon bus operations for many years to come. The Leyland Atlantean provided greater passenger capacity, and at the same time made one-man operation of double-decker buses a possibility in the longer term. The first to put the new bus into use was Wallasey Corporation, and 30 were purchased with bodywork by Met-Cammell. No. 5 is at New Brighton in September 1964, bound for Seacombe Ferry.

Changes in passenger and staff requirements caused some operators to abandon the traditional open rear platform during the 1950s, and to equip their vehicles with platform doors. No doors were provided on the first three vehicles of a 1958 delivery of Leyland PD3/4 buses to Merthyr Tydfil Corporation, but the last two buses of the order were fitted with fully enclosed platforms as part of their East Lancashire bodywork. No. 104 of this latter type is seen in Merthyr in September 1964 followed, somewhat ominously, by the Corporation breakdown tender.

1964 saw the Diamond Jubilee of public transport operation in Maidstone, and to mark the occasion No. 14, a 1959 Leyland PD2/30 with Massey bodywork, was decorated with flags and insignia. This colourfully-finished vehicle is seen in July by the Queen's Monument in the town centre.

Massey bodywork was also provided on this Leyland PD2/40 delivered to Birkenhead Corporation in 1961. No. 43 stands in the entrance to New Ferry Garage in May 1965 flanked by a smart-looking collection of Guy and Leyland double-deckers.

A scene in the South Wales town of Caerphilly, where No. 29 of the Urban District Council fleet is seen near the famous castle. The Leyland PD3/4 has Massey low height bodywork, and was some two years old when this photograph was taken in June 1963. Note the destination winding equipment to the left of the driver's cab.

Wigan Corporation vehicles usually possessed a well-cared-for appearance, and this Leyland PD3A/2 with forward entrance body by Massey is no exception, although it is here seen enjoying a rare visit to the County of Kent. New in 1962, No.49 was photographed in Knightrider Street, Maidstone, in January 1964 working on a trolleybus service to the Bull Inn at Barming.

Teesside Railless Traction Board was one of the last municipal operators to remain faithful to the trolleybus, but it also possessed a substantial number of buses operated from a small depot at Cargo Fleet. Leyland PD2/27 No. 26 of 1959 is equipped with a Roe body and is seen in the depot yard in January 1968. Note the destination legend.

The prize for the largest destination screens provided at both front and rear in these pages must go to this Guy Otter with Mulliner bodywork, one of five supplied to Douglas Corporation in 1957. Seen in September 1967, No. 9 is passing Villa Marina on Douglas promenade and is bound for Victoria Pier Bus Station. Compare this vehicle with the former LT GS Class on page 62.

The Guy Wulfrunian was a very rare animal indeed outside the West Riding of Yorkshire, and in municipal circles examples were only operated by Accrington, Bury and Wolverhampton. The Accrington vehicles were the only ones built with rear entrances, and No. 157 is depicted in Accrington town centre in September 1965 en route to Oswaldtwistle. The two operated by Accrington were new in 1961 and were bodied by East Lancashire; they were both withdrawn in 1968 and scrapped in 1971 after a life of only ten years.

The Albion motif is clearly visible on this forward entrance Leyland PD3/2, supplied new to Glasgow Corporation in 1961 and equipped with bodywork by the purchaser. No. L363 is passing along Argyle Street beneath the famous 'Highlandmans Umbrella' formed by the railway bridge at Central station; May 1965.

Chester Corporation
was one of the select
few operators to take
delivery of Guy Arab
IV vehicles with the
so-called
'Johannesburg' front.
No. 29 dates from
1961 and has Massey
bodywork. It is seen in
October 1963 passing
beneath the Eastgate.

▶

As in the case of
Sheffield,
Huddersfield also
possessed a fleet in
which some vehicle
were in joint
ownership with
British Railways,
whilst others were
entirely the propert
of the Corporation.
the Joint Omnibus
Committee fleet,
alternate vehicles
carried Corporatio
and British Railway
legal ownership
lettering, whilst the
buses in the
Corporation camp
could be recognised
because they sporte
'streamlined' style o
livery, as seen in thi
photograph. This
smart Roe-bodied
Leyland PD3A/2 w
new to the
Corporation in 196
and is seen in this
illustration standing
outside the railway
station in August
1963.

Belfast Corporation owned a most interesting and varied fleet of buses, including some experimental types purchased for evaluation. This photograph shows the sole Leyland Atlantean in the fleet, introduced in 1960 and bodied by Alexander. It was caught by the camera in March 1968 when passing York Road station bound for Turf Lodge.

The Bridgemaster was an A E C type which did not find many buyers in the municipal field. Cardiff purchased six in 1960 for which Park Royal provided the bodies. One of these, No. 364, is seen in June 1963 in Caerphilly when working the long trunk route from Cardiff to Tredegar.

Minibuses have never been commonplace on the municipal scene, but were used by Aberdare and Wallasey at least. The former is represented by No.9, a Morris with thirteen seats, introduced in 1962; photographed at Victoria Square, Aberdare, in September 1964.

The new order is demonstrated by this A E C Reliance with dual-door Duple body supplied to Reading Corporation in 1962. Seen in July of the following year outside the garage at Mill Lane, this 34-seat bus was designed for one-man operation, and for the carriage of 26 standee passengers. Note the tram lines still present at Mill Lane in this photograph.

The Halifax Joint Committee operated this Leyland PD2/37 with Weymann bodywork delivered in 1962, and seen in February 1967 at Outlane in the suburbs of Huddersfield.

Walsall Corporation could usually be relied upon to provide vehicles of special interest. Daimler Fleetline No. 1 was a short (25' 7") vehicle with Northern Counties body, and with the entrance to the rear of the front axle. It had been exhibited at the Commercial Motor Show in 1962 before entering service. Walsall Bus Station; May 1968.

Atkinson single-decker vehicles saw service with Sunderland Corporation, and this Marshall-bodied example entered traffic in 1963. It is seen in High Street, Sunderland, on a wet September day in 1965, and again shows the two-door boarding/alighting system then beginning to find favour.

Below; equally rare is this Daimler Freeline of Great Yarmouth, new in 1962. Bodywork is by Roe and the scene is the South Denes terminus of Route 4 in August 1964.

The Leyland PD2/24 was still in demand by Swindon Corporation when this vehicle was purchased in 1962 and equipped with Weymann bodywork; No.128 looks extremely smart in July 1964.

Delivered new in 1964, this Wigan Corporation Leyland PD2A/27 has Northern Counties bodywork, and is seen outside Wigan Central station in September 1966. Compare with the Massey-bodied vehicle on loan to Maidstone on page 77.

By 1963, five years after the initial delivery to Wallasey Corporation, the Leyland Atlantean had made its mark on the roads of the United Kingdom. This example with Met-Cammell body was delivered in that year to Bury Corporation, and is seen at Rawtenstall Bus Station in April 1969.

Despite the changes in design taking place in the early 1960s, Chester Corporation kept faith with the more traditional Guy Arab V, and No.34, dating from 1963 and equipped with Massey bodywork, is seen passing Chester Castle on a bright winter's day in January 1967. In 1969, Chester Corporation was the last operator in the United Kingdom to take delivery of Guy Arab vehicles.

Wolverhampton, perhaps naturally, was a staunch supporter of Guy Motors Ltd. Introduced in 1963, this Arab V with Weymann body is seen at the Castlecroft terminus of Route 43 towards the end of October 1967. The vehicle has an A E C A V590 engine.

e have seen the Albion motif
rth of the border with Glasgow
orporation, but ten examples of
e Lowlander design were put
to service by Southend
orporation, being provided
th Alexander bodies. No.328
presents this type, and was
otographed when new in May
63 at Prittlewell Works,
uthend. The ex-LT Daimlers
ongside have turned their last
eel in passenger service.

The Daimler answer to the Leyland Atlantean was the rear-engined Fleetline, and the type was destined to make a major breakthrough into bus fleets generally. This early example for Sunderland Corporation was delivered in 1962 and has a Roe body, with the Daimler motif common to the earlier deliveries of Fleetline chassis; Sunderland station, April 1964.

Making a first appearance in these pages, this Leyland Leopard was purchased by West Hartlepool Corporation in 1964. It has Strachan bodywork and is seen at West Hartlepool in September 1965 awaiting the next call to duty.

Bodywork on this Leyland Leopard L2 is by Massey, and it also dates from 1964, making an interesting contrast with the West Hartlepool one above. Birkenhead Corporation No. 94 (at Haymarket in May 1965) was one of four single-deckers owned by the Corporation at that period.

Newcastle Central station is the scene for this Leyland Atlantean, which is leaving the stops on the opposite side of the road to the station facade. No.44 has Alexander bodywork and was brand new in April 1964 when seen on Route 45.

Also new in 1964 were two Daimler Fleetline vehicles with bodywork by M H Coachworks. Originally intended for Belfast Corporation, they were diverted to Bournemouth; No.40 negotiates busy Christchurch Road in August during its first summer season on the south coast.

Lancaster City Transport took delivery of this Leyland PD2/37 with East Lancashire body in 1965. It is seen in June of that year in Market Street.

Below: Lincoln Corporation first purchased rear-engined vehicles in 1964, when four Leyland Atlanteans with Roe bodies were put into service. Seen in May 1965, No. 97 is approaching the Eastgate on Route 12.

Nottingham City Transport frequently adopts a body styling which is distinctive to the vehicles of that city, and No.425 is an example of Met–Cammell bodies delivered on Leyland Atlantean PDR1/2 chassis in 1965. The vehicle is in St. Annes Well Road in August 1965 en route to Bulwell Hall Estate.

This final scene on the Isle of Man features the first sight in these pages of a Bedford VAS1. Two of these were purchased with Duple bodies and put to work in 1966. They were often to be found working Route 15 to Port Soderick, where No.6 is arriving in September 1967.

Birmingham City Transport introduced some Daimler Fleetline chassis in 1965 with single-decker bodies by Marsha The buses were used on one-ma operated services, and No.3469 pulling away from a stop in Linden Road, Bournville, in September 1966 whilst workin Route 27C.

Another chassis type to appear at this late stage is that of Ford, and No.720 of Wolverhampton Corporation is shown leaving the terminus at the High Level station in September 1967. Delivered a year earlier, this Ford R226 has 54-seat bodywork by Strachan.

94

Trolleybus replacement in Maidstone brought the first use of rear-engined vehicles to the Corporation fleet. Seen when new in December 1965, No. 31 has Massey bodywork on Leyland Atlantean Mark II chassis, and is closely followed along Knightrider Street by a Guy Arab of East Kent.

Sheffield Corporation was interesting because the fleet was split into three goups, each being owned entirely by the Corporation, entirely by British Railways or jointly. Daimler Fleetline No. 109 of Sheffield Corporation leaving the Central Bus Station in August 1967 on Route 4. Bodywork is by Park Royal and the vehicle entered service in 1965. It is a member of the Corporation-owned 'A' fleet.

Towards the end of the decade many smaller municipalities were entering their final years of existence as independent operators. Darwen, for example, was to be swallowed up by Blackburn in 1974, but in July 1968, when this Leyland PD2A/27 was photographed at Darwen Circus, this final day of reckoning was still some time ahead. Delivered in 1967, No. 38 has bodywork by East Lancashire.

95

In 1967 Chesterfield Corporation took delivery of a batch of Daimler Roadliners with 49-seat East Lancashire bodies, built by Neepsend Coachworks. Representing this type when new, No. 75 is seen outside the bus station during August of its first year in service. These vehicles were 36′ long, and featured fixed glazing, double-glazed roof panels and low height bell pushes for use by children.

By the end of the 1960s, the municipal bus scene had changed dramatically from that commonplace ten years earlier. The single-decker with underfloor or rear-mounted engine had appeared in numerous fleets, but the double-decker was poised to make an early return to favour in the new one-man operated role. The final scene in this volume depicts an A E C Swift with Willowbrook bodywork supplied to Gelligaer Urban District Council in 1968. Seen outside the garage in New Road, Hengoed, in June 1969, the appearance of No. 38 in red, white and green livery is a credit to the management and staff of the undertaking.